For Tyler Widney,
one of my 2nd graders,
who gave me the title and idea for this book
—T.L.

For Charlie, Maggie, Zoe, and Connor
—C.J.

Publisher's Cataloging-in-Publication
(Provided by Quality Books, Inc.)

Lish, Ted.
    The three little puppies and the big bad flea/
Ted Lish ; illustrated by Charles Jordan. -- 1st
ed.
    p.cm.
    SUMMARY: Three puppies leave home as they are
warned about the Big Bad Flea. They build houses
using flimsy materials, which the flea knocks down
easily.
    LCCN: 00-100359
    ISBN: 0-7940-0000-2 (hc)
    ISBN: 0-7940-0001-0 (lib. bdg.)

    1. Puppies--Juvenile fiction. 2. Fleas--
Juvenile fiction. 3. Three little pigs--Parodies,
imitations, etc. I. Jordan, Charles.
II. Title

PZ7.L674Thr 2001   [E]
                  QB100-275

Printed in Hong Kong • First Printing June 2001
Second Printing July 2001

3 5 7 9 10 8 6 4 2

Typeset in Stone Informal.
Typography by Pete Masterson, www.aeonix.com.
Jacket design by Bookwrights Design.
Illustrations were done in colored pencil and ink.

The Three Little Puppies and the Big Bad Flea

by Ted Lish

illustrated by Charles Jordan

Munchweiler Press

Victorville, California

nce upon a time, there were three little puppies who decided it was time to leave home.

"Don't worry about cats," shouted mama as they were leaving, "but watch out for the big bad flea!"

"Ha! Ha! Ha!" laughed the three little puppies.
"Who ever heard of a big bad flea?"
So off they went to seek their fortunes.

Soon they came to a duck farm. "I like my featherbed so much that I'm going to build my house out of duck feathers," said the first little puppy. The ducks were more than happy to give her a ton of duck feathers (and that's a lot of feathers).

So she set out happily to build a very fine duck feather house.

The other two little puppies continued their journey and soon came to a nice forest with lots of leaves on the ground.

"I like to play in the leaves so much that I'm going to build my house out of leaves," said the second little puppy.

Well, the leaves were there for the taking, so she gathered up a ton of them (and that's a lot of leaves, too).

So she set out happily to build a very fine leaf house.

The third little puppy continued her journey and soon came to a cobbler's shop.

The cobbler just happened to be throwing away lots and lots of old shoes, and was more than happy to give them to the third little puppy (and what puppy doesn't like old shoes?).

So the third little puppy carried away tons and tons of old shoes, and set out happily to build a very fine old shoe house.

Each little puppy was enjoying her new house when along came the Big Bad Flea. She just loved biting little puppies. Even big dogs would scatter and run away when they saw the Big Bad Flea coming!

The first house she came to was the house made of duck feathers. She knew there was a puppy inside so she knocked on the door and said, "Little Puppy, Little Puppy, I know you're in there. Open the door and let me come in."

The first little puppy thought, *"Now who can that be?"* So she peeped through the peep hole and saw a gigantic flea! And of course, she looked even bigger through the peep hole!

"Yikes!" said the first little puppy, "Mama wasn't kidding! You're not coming in here by all fifty hairs on my chinny chin chin!"

"Then I'll huff and I'll puff and I'll blow your house in!" shouted the Big Bad Flea. So she huffed and she puffed and she blew the house in. (It was easy, even for a flea.)

The first little puppy just barely escaped (with only a few painful bites on her backside) and ran straight to the second little puppy's leaf house. She told her sister all about the Big Bad Flea.

"Oh dear! Oh dear!" cried the second little puppy. "We should have listened to mama!" So they bolted the door and hid under the bed.

Just then the Big Bad Flea began pounding on the door, shouting, "Little Puppies, Little Puppies, open the door and let me come in!" "Not by all one hundred hairs on our chinny chin chins!" cried the very scared little puppies.

"Then I'll huff and I'll puff and I'll blow your house in!" shouted the Big Bad Flea. So she huffed and she puffed and she blew the house in (almost as easily as the duck feather house).

The little puppies just barely escaped (with only a few painful bites on their backsides), and ran straight to the third little puppy's old shoe house.

Once inside, the terrified little puppies bolted the door and excitedly told the third little puppy all about the Big Bad Flea. "Don't worry," said the third little puppy. "No flea can blow this house down!"

But guess who came knocking at the door? Yep. It was none other than the Big Bad Flea, shouting, "Little Puppies, Little Puppies, open the door and let me come in!"

"Not by all one hundred fifty hairs on our chinny chin chins!" answered the now brave three little puppies.

"Then I'll huff and I'll puff and I'll blow your house in!" shouted the Big Bad Flea. So she huffed and she puffed and she puffed and she huffed, but even the Big Bad Flea couldn't blow down a house made of old shoes.

"Well," said the Big Bad Flea to herself, "I'm not going down the chimney and get cooked in a pot like that dumb old wolf did. I'll just sneak in through the key hole."

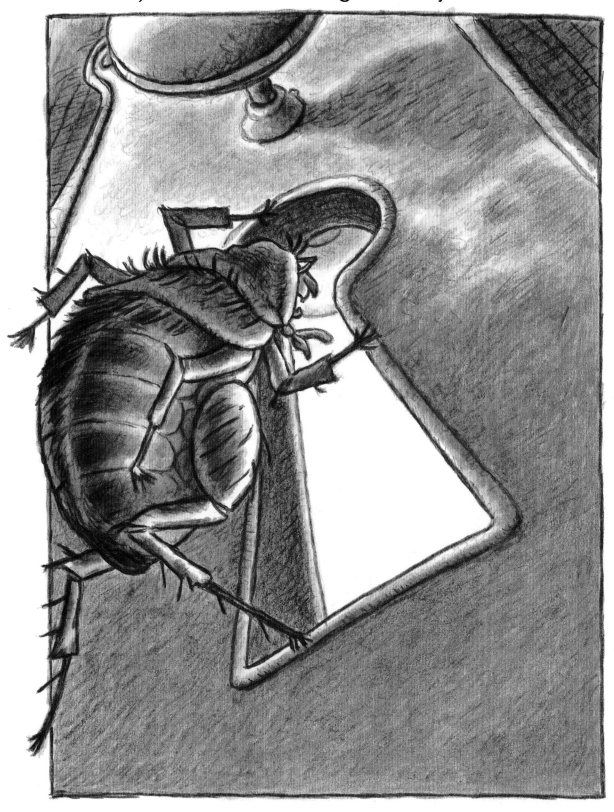

So she climbed in through the key hole and chased the three little puppies all around, biting them on the backside, biting them on the neck, biting them all over,

until they ran yelping and howling out the back door!

The Big Bad Flea liked her new old shoe house so much that she decided to stay there and raise a family. She had billions and billions of children. (There were lots of old shoes for them to sleep in.)

Soon all the little flea children left home and went looking for dogs. And they all found dogs, and started bugging them. And they're still bugging them to this very day!

As for the Three Little Puppies? They learned a valuable lesson about listening to their mama, and moved far, far away from the Big Bad Flea!

Publisher's Note:
We're very sorry, but sometimes
the Munchweiler elves like to hide in the pictures.
Just ignore them.

(See the Munchweiler elves at www.munchweilerpress.com)

(Six elves hidden in pictures.)

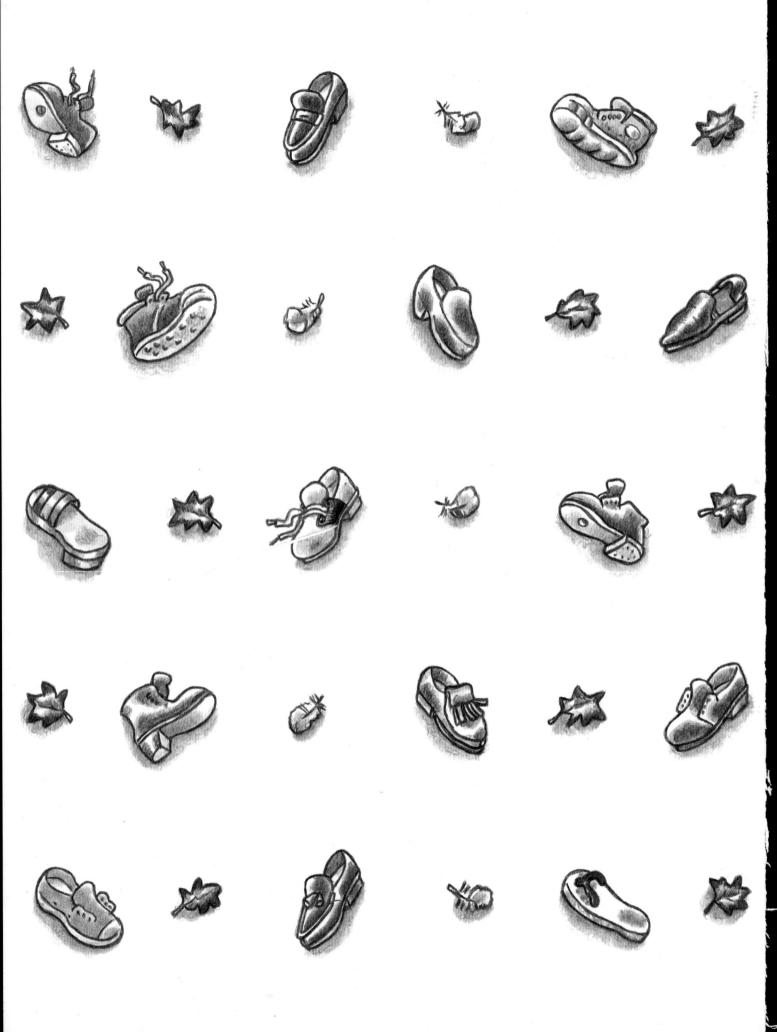